I0504584

TABLE OF CONTENTS

Moving Out, Working Abroad and Keeping Your Sanity

11 secrets to make your expat life better than you imagine

Levi Borba

Expat, Entrepreneur and founder of Colligere Expat Consultancy (expatriateconsultancy.com)

2020

Copyright © 2020
All rights reserved

To the pioneers, navigators, seekers and finders
Dedicated to those that defined boundaries
Without losing sight of their origins.

FOREWORD

What bad can happen when you are far from home?

Stress may be common even in minor situations like buying a bus ticket. Finance can be a problem, especially when living costs hugely differ - either you get carried by the spending frenzy with smaller prices, or the higher bills make you feel ripped by everyone around. Being away from family, friends and people you love may make you crouch in your bed and see everything in shades of blue.

Adjusting to a new culture demands a lot of energy, and at some point is downright exhausting! Lonely is overwhelming after some time - even though at the beginning you may not feel it - and language barriers can make it even worse. Simple things like choosing a cereal bar are a challenge when the language barrier strikes and you end buying dog food.

And then come all those stories of the neighborhood kids leaving the country just to come back a year or two later in total despair, after facing the solitude and inclemency of this brave new world.

I had been there. Almost a decade ago I left my small city, a place with air smelling like orange cake and parrots waking me up in the morning. Then when I was getting used to my new home, 390 km farther, I moved again, over three thousand kilometers away. And then, only one year later, again, for a 14-hour-flight distance. Three years later, another move, now almost an entire day by airplane travel and half a planet far from everyone I grew with.

Every time farther.

Still, here I am, alive, carrying now a complete world of experiences, new relationships, priceless lessons, and a big scar in my feet (the last one is not necessarily related).

Some experiences that I will tell in this book will look unpleasant at first glance, but I would not change them for anything! I changed, however, some names involved since few stories are quite embarrassing.

Moving out is, at some point, uncomfortable. There is no way to bypass this sensation, but the whole reason I am writing this book is because it is possible to be comfortable with the idea of being uncomfortable! At some point, you will even enjoy it.

This is not a book of simple hacks nor practical solutions. First, because there are plenty of it on the internet, and second because they differ vastly between countries. A useful life hack in London can be useless in New York. It may not even be useful in Liverpool, which is only 2 hours away!

This book is rather about universal concerns: the mental

preparation, the struggle with homesickness, the adaptation to the hustle and bustle of a new life. This book is to help you to not be that person rescued by parents from a depressing experience abroad. It is a book to turn you into the uncle or cousin whose visits everyone expects and always comes with exotic gifts and exciting news.

So pack your luggage, take your tickets and let's move.

EXPAT OR IMMIGRANT?

It was a scorching morning in Qatar (just like almost all the other mornings in that country), still during my first year living in the Arabian Peninsula. I was sharing an apartment with an Argentinian called Matteo, slightly older than me. Every morning we went to work together, and this day he told me about his weekend in Dubai. He said the biggest difference between where we lived (Doha) and there was that in Dubai he had the impression of seeing fewer immigrants and more expats like us.

I got surprised by those words. Not by Matteo's impression itself, but for the fact I thought immigrants and expats are the same thing, just like spouse and wife, or downtown and city center. Apparently, it was not.

Digging into the meaning of the two words, I realized that "expats", in that context, meant white-collar professionals and westerners with qualified jobs. On the other side, "immigrants" were construction and domestic workers. They made around 70% of Qatar's population, and the majority of them came from the Indian subcontinent, Egypt, and the Philippines.

To be honest, I never attached myself to this difference because later in life, while starting my business, I done both types of jobs. Maybe the word expat has a more temporary sense than the permanent aspect implied by "immigrant". But on the other side there are plenty of cases of expats moving to another country just as a step in their corporate careers, but suddenly they meet the love of their lives - or any other great opportunity - and boom! Nothing is provisional anymore.

The temporary aspect plays a big role when you are an expat (or an immigrant). Some people imagine this change as similar to changing jobs. It is not. When you move from one company to another, you change what you will do 8 or 9 hours per day. When you move abroad, it is a around the clock, seven days per week transformation. This change comes with burdens not found when you just move from one office to another.

You leave behind friends and family, and though some of them may visit you depending on the distance, the costs of keeping personal contact can be unbearable and you should not expect to have many visits overseas. You will see your baby nephew grow up only via social media. You will miss them, and although the web improved connectivity, the different time zones will create periods of the day when there is no one back home to talk with (except insomniacs or early birds). Those are some less glittering aspects of living abroad, and you must have guts to start over and prepare yourself. The good thing is that I am here to tell you how decade-long expats faced these challenges.

The expatriate roller coaster

To write this book, besides my years living abroad, I also got inspiration from few external sources. From Individuals I highly admire for their resilience when facing some of the most diverse obstacles in life out of their countries. Living abroad, eventually you will need to choose between two groups of acquaintances: the first complains about everything they do not have in their new country; the second thrives with what they have in hand. Choose the second. They may even inspire you to write a book as I did!

A constant in the life of expatriates that already spent years overseas is what I call the expatriate roller coaster. This ride, just as the one in amusement parks, builds on emotional stages that virtually all expatriate goes through. The duration of each stage depends on circumstances and backgrounds, but at some point, you will identify yourself in each of the steps.

1.   Stage: Honeymoon – Everything looks beautiful. You still have touristy eyes, and you see so many things better than back home! You discover which typical dishes are the most enjoyable and chooses a favorite local food. You even think, "Oh Dear, I could live just eating this!" - It is what came to my mind after trying Oscypek. The duration of this stage normally depends of how different are your original and your new country. In my experience, the stage one takes from a few months to one year.

2.   Stage: Annoyance – The small daily nuisances if isolated

would do no harm. However, they begin to accumulate like some oriental torture. Petty bureaucracies, difficulty to understand the local behavior, problems to send a letter at the local post office, or to do a quick shop at the nearby convenience store. All sums up and gives way to negative feelings. You start to miss your typical holidays.

If these small drops of frustration pile up, they turn into feelings like sadness, embitterment or homesickness. This stage can take a year or more, and often people give up and return home right here. This is why, during my time in the Middle East, we saw a considerable number of "anniversary resignations", people leaving just after completing their first year.

3.   Stage: Acceptance – If you were resilient enough to survive the stage two, the previous adversities start to soften by continuous learning about the modus operandi of your new home. You begin to understand that there are other ways to live. You learn to compromise minor things like changing fish for bacon or Açai for Cranberries. You may even start to get the local language, and this will open an entire universe of discoveries and possibilities. The obstacles from the previous phase start to look smaller. On the other hand, homesickness and nostalgia can reappear with the violence of tropical thunderstorms, and this is the reason some expats also give up here.

4.   Stage: Satisfaction – You are almost settled, albeit there are still noticeable differences to home. Those differences will ever be there anyway, but you learned how to endure and adapt to them. You can navigate the local bureaucracy almost like a na-

tive and start to be part of the local community. You may even have a close friendship or a romance with someone you met after moving.

5.   Stage: Yearning – Also known as re-adaptation. It comes with the notion you got attached to your new place and now that you are moving somewhere else, you will even miss it. Some people think this happens only with expats returning to their home country, but it is not true. Every time I moved from one location to the next, besides missing my homeland, I felt nostalgia for other countries I lived. So, even if you return to your motherland, to the same street where you played as a kid, you may feel as a foreigner.

The people you met before moved on, things are not in the same places as before. It is impossible to meet my high school friends in the same bowling bar as in my teenager years because it is now a veterinary center. That is when you realize you made it! You also moved on! We will remember those experiences we went through with a smile on our faces.

And everything will be just fine.

RULE ONE: DEFINE WHICH KIND OF EXPAT YOU ARE

There are plenty of questions to answer when you are moving out:

- Will my money, or salary, be enough?

- Where will I live?

- Can I speak their language, or at least learn it without headache?

- What will I do with my belongings? Should I sell or ship it?

- What about the bureaucracy or the visa procedures?

- What should I do in case of getting sick or needing emergency care?

I had been at this situation several times in my life and at the end of this book you will be able to solve most of those questions. Here I will teach you the mental and social tools to find the answers. The very first step is to learn which kind of expatriate you are. After you learn to identify what is your type, it may shock you to know that people move abroad without thinking about it! It may be the reason so many of them come back frustrated.

Periodically the network InterNations promotes The Expat Insider[1], one of the biggest worldwide surveys about immigration and emigration. They made a convenient division of the expats in 6 types:

1.   The Optimizer: Representing 16% of the total, they moved for a better quality of life, finances, political, religious or safety reasons. The majority of them are men (56%) and are in a relationship (66%).

2.   The Explorer: They make 12% of the total, and moved because of the appeal of life abroad, or because they were looking for new adventures and challenges. Their numbers are quite balanced between men and women, and just a small minority have children.

3.   The Foreign Assignee: Making 10% of the expats, they went abroad by request of their existing employers, and the large majority of them are men in a relationship.

4.   The Go-Getter: Representing 21% of the respondents, they moved out to start their business, find a job, or were recruited locally. The majority are well-educated men in a relation-

ship.

5.   The Travelling Spouse: This 8% of the whole expat community are the ones moved to follow their partners. If most of the types until now are male-dominated, here women are an absolute majority: 86%.

6.   The Romantic: The last category represents 12%[2] of the total. They moved to the country of their partners. Mostly are women in a relationship, but there are a significant number of men in this category (me included).

One interesting thing here is that the categories are not definitive. There are plenty of cases where Foreign Assignees become Go-Getters when they spot an opportunity and change from employees to employers. The Romantic also often is part of another category besides their current one.

When I moved to Chile, I was a Foreign Assignee, the same as when I moved to Qatar. My life in Poland started as a Romantic, but almost after arrival, I also turned into a Go-Getter by starting my business. Henceforth, categories should not limit or make you think you will always belong to only one of them. Eventually, expatriates will move from one to the other.

Have in mind that each of those types have their goals and dreams. Each of them have also their advantages and disadvantages. A Travelling Spouse or the Romantic may not feel as alone as an Explorer, while the Foreign Assignee, with the guaranteed income source from his job, will take less risk. We will talk more about the pros and cons in this book.

There is also a type not represented above in any category: individuals moving away to evade their families and domestic problems. My best guess for their absence is because they are short-lived. When you move away to escape from your private problems, you will not solve them at all. You are just making it even more difficult to solve them by distance when it gets unbearable.

There is another important characteristic you will discover when understanding your type: if you are a provisional or long-lasting expat. The first is someone planning to live abroad for a certain, pre-established number of years. The second is a person who is moving out with a long-term plan or permanently. A foreign-assignee or explorer most likely will be a provisional, unless they fall in love with a local or start their own business, becoming, respectively, a romantic or go-getter, two long-lasting types.

Are your plans in your new country temporary or long-term? Are you moving out just to progress in your career and then return home with a bigger salary or are you willing to build a new life outside? The first secret of this book is to know yourself by answering those questions. You cannot follow the other rules, especially the number 2 and 3, before defining who you are. You cannot research what is better for you or what are your goals if you don't know what you are looking for. The answer to these questions not only will make you feel more comfortable and secure, but they will be a basis for a better expat life.

Ask yourself why you are leaving. Ask yourself if you are planning to come back soon. Then, you will have self-knowledge enough to the next steps.

RULE TWO- DO A PROPER RESEARCH, NOT A MEDIA- BASED ONE

During the time I lived in Doha, most of the company staff were foreigners. It was just a reflection of the country demographic, largely made of immigrants[3]. Still, there were almost no other Brazilians like me, except the boss of the boss of my boss. There were some certain rumors about Brazilians not resisting much time there because of the vast distance to their country, plus the enormous cultural differences. To my surprise, just a few months after they hire me, they also hired a fellow national called Breno.

Breno had a respectable curriculum. Graduated is the USA, in one of the top universities in his area, worked for the pride-company of the Brazilian aerospace industry and despite being young (he was just slightly older than I was), had a list of achievements uncommon for his age. He also looked slightly like a frat-boy coming out from a B-class American comedy. Very easy-going person, making funny jokes about all things.

In one of his first days, I was at my desk calibrating some technical parameters, and Breno comes to me and ask:

Hey Levi! What's up? What about we go for some drinks?

Qatar was not an easy country to go for some drinks. It was illegal to sell alcohol in all stores except one, which was state-owned and demanded a special license to buy their 300% overpriced booze. They also sold alcoholic drinks at bars and restaurants of luxury hotels. There, a round of cocktails could cost as much as a weekend on a Greek beach, hotel included.

Despite being busy, the question of Breno surprised me, since at the beginning you don't have so much money to spare, at least until receive your first salary. Did he know the alcohol was so expensive there? Maybe he found someone with a license to buy alcoholic drinks and was giving a house party? The guy was so easygoing, it would not be a surprise.

No. It was nothing like that. He had another idea in mind, which I discovered when I asked where he wanted to go.

"Maybe we can go to the party district! Where is it? You know, this street full of bars and clubs that every big city in the world has!"

That is it. He just asked me about a Bangkok style party district in an Islamic society where a woman could face problems if their skirts were above their knees. A place where was often cheaper to buy an airline ticket to another country if you wanted to party.

This guy had no idea where he was.

The story of Breno may sound odd, but it is not uncommon. There are plenty of people that don't make a proper field research before moving. Or when they make, they use only media sources, with information written by journalists. Some of those journalists act almost as public relations from governments, publishing information that is unrealistic or exaggeratedly welcoming.

Maybe Breno imagined Doha as a middle-eastern Barcelona because he saw so many media vehicles praising Qatar for having less strict Islamic rules when compared to Saudi Arabia. Yes, it is less strict, but what the media omitted is that Saudi is the strictest Islamic country in the world. To be less, in this case, is natural. When Qatar earned the right to host the football World Cup, there was plenty of government money going around. Maybe that is why journalists felt compelled to do unrealistic and overoptimistic comparisons, like between Doha and Dubai.

I cannot stress enough how important is to do proper research before moving out, and I am sure most expats do it. However, unfortunately, they just do not do it right. Go to the easiest source of information (newspapers, internet portals or YouTube videos) is not a good idea. Editors, presenters and reporters are not there to help someone to live abroad but to earn a living, so they may just create content to draw attention. Sensationalist talks.

This is something that I saw in Poland. More often than never I witnessed in expat forums questions about how safe is for a dark-skinned person to walk in the polish streets. The answer, from my side, is elementary: as safe as you can imagine. The number of racist assaults in Poland is negligible and even being an olive-skinned guy and knowing plenty of Afro-Brazilians, I still didn't hear about this kind of problem. So, why people fear those hordes of racist poles which, in over three years here, I did not saw? Because they write about it in the media, they show it on the TV, and it may be one of the first things you see when you type Poland at Google. However, all this repetition does not make it true.

The difference between what the press portrays and street reality can be abysmal. So if I am telling here that the main media vehicles are not the best source to research your new country, where should you seek information? Can you guess?

The real people. The ones who went through the same experiences and endured it for years. Thanks to the same web I criticized above, you also can reach them easily.

Social media today is full of groups. They often have names as "Foreigners in [name of the place]". I don't recommend these groups as the sole source of information because many of their members are expats still in their honeymoon phase (see previous chapters) or just tourists. But while they cannot provide you with the most reliable information, it is still better than the traditional media.

The real deal is to look for groups of locals. One easy way I found is to find language learning groups in the country where I am moving too. Not only you will be able to communicate with locals from your new country and learn their idiom, but they will be excited if you offer to teach them your language. It can be fun too!

Another possibility is to look for common interests. Even before moving to Europe, I was already in local groups about entrepreneurship, football and philosophy, three subjects interesting to me. While discussing things I enjoyed, I learned about local views on those subjects and other common topics. If you are already in the country but feeling you don't know enough about it - since most of your contacts are foreigners - enrolling in a course or volunteering can be useful and pleasant.

A third way is to find people from your new country that now are living where you live. You can do that on social media. For example, if you are a Canadian moving to Argentina, you can just look on Facebook for the group "Argentinians in Canada" (or, most likely, Argentinos en Canadá). The members know how is to be a foreigner and will be glad to help with your doubts about their country.

After I told you where to look for information, comes the next question: Which information should you seek?

Questions to ask

Most of the first questions when moving out are about living costs, language, bureaucracy, etc.

For this reason, many groups of foreigners at social media will already have a FAQ or index for questions like:

How long it takes to have my resident card?

What is the best health insurance?

Which cellphone company is better?

In my consulting firm (Colligere Expat Consultancy, you can find us at http://expatriateconsultancy.com/) those are the reasons most expats come to us to help them.

I will not reply to those questions here. Not only because they differ from country to country, but also because it is straightforward to find those answers since they are the things everyone asks. The way to find those answers is the same explained previously: ask the locals in social media. Or, if you are moving to one of the countries my consultancy supports, you have a 20-minute free-consultation with us at Colligere.

However, there is another group of questions, which often nobody asks. Because nobody takes interests in these questions, so many expats experience frustration and regret. The questions I am talking about are the same that Breno should have asked before going to Qatar. They are about cultural shock.

The Dutch psychologist Geert Hofstede[4] organized a study of national cultures using group dimensions which should quantify the core values of a society. Hofstede's research examines national and organizational settings. In doing so, it traces a general guideline about how different cultures would act in social and work environments. His study let us compare the cultural attitude of different countries, including the one we are living in and the one we are moving to.

Few fields can cause cultural shock, and four of the most significant are[5]:

1st – **The Rules**. The approach to rules and regulations can be significantly different between certain nations. Germanic and Japanese cultures, on one side, value procedures, systems and control, focusing on getting things done how they were planned. On the other side, romance cultures like Iberians or Italians give greater value to ad hoc problem-solving, relationship building and adaptation to circumstances. Now you can imagine how misunderstandings can appear when a Swiss border officer questions a laid back Latin-American student, or an Austrian client can be impatient in a Portuguese café because the waiter is talking too much.

2nd – **The Time**. This is one of the earliest sources of cultural shock. I experienced it profoundly. The different perceptions of time can make an inexperienced expat deeply frustrated and be a common source of friction. In Latin-American cultures, punctuality is not that important for social gatherings or informal occasions. An Anglophone that shows exactly as invited, for example, at 9 PM for a party or at 8 AM for the company breakfast, may find himself completely alone in the room and confused. In the same way, it surprised my wife that in Brazil was not a problem to arrive at a doctor's appointment five minutes late (because the doctor would just call my name ten minutes later).

Understanding how society handles deadlines is useful to your professional life. Contrary to some stereotypes, laid back nationalities like Greeks and Mexicans are among those making more over-hours on the planet, while Germans are the ones doing less. Try to seek more information about how the people of your new country deal with time, how strict they are with deadlines, and if the dentist will still see you if you are five minutes late. This analysis will be very useful to you sooner than you can imagine.

3rd – **The Humor**. Some cultures, like the Irish or Latin Americans, have humor as a constant component of their behavior, and jokes may surge even when things are not going well. Others, like the British, may use humor as a conversation starter, to break the ice or even to grant some loans from the US to save their economy (like princess Margaret did in 1965[6]). At the other side, jokes at Swiss business meetings can backfire because they may see it as a waste of time. In Slavic countries, to laugh with people that didn't get the joke, may give the signal as you are laughing at them. I cannot recount how many times people asked me in Poland why I was laughing for things like a baby throwing his cap on the floor (you should see, it was funny).

4th – **The Communication**. As the consultancy firm Expatica explained in their page: *Different communication styles can be a ticking time-bomb, especially in the workplace. Plenty of cultures prefer to engage in lengthy hypothetical discussions with few concrete conclusions. A meeting with French colleagues, for instance, might lack structure or even an agenda altogether. Others prefer discussions with a clear and well-defined structure that allows participants to compartmentalize everything said. People who speak with a great deal of ambiguity or subtlety in their speech (the British are notorious here) may frustrate those that prefer clear and direct communication, though they may also impress their colleagues that have trouble working out complicated situations.*

So, here we come to the question made some paragraphs ago: to do proper research goes beyond asking about internet providers and insurance plans, you must also know those cultural shock differences. Preferably before you arrive or as soon as you land in your new country. If you are already living abroad, it is still a very interesting exercise and you can discover a lot by doing it.

Extra Content – The Curious differences of a smile in Slavic and Latin-American countries.

This article had a good repercussion in my Medium profile (medium.com/@leviborba). It exemplifies the degree of cultural shock between Eastern Europe and South-America. If you are not interested in any of those two regions of the world–you do not know what you are missing–you can jump straight to the "Questions to ask yourself"

> *An innocent smile is enough to make people*
> *think you are not taking them seriously.*

Smiling may look like a trivial gesture for most of my kind. Born in the Brazilian countryside, I learned from the beginning that it was not weird to smile to strangers in the streets. I am not talking about Joker-Style creepy laughs, but about those gracious expressions of friendliness, usually accompanied by a nod. We salute our neighbors, co-workers and, on a good day, anyone that crosses our way.

The same applied to the first country that I lived after leaving Brazil — Chile — and to others I visited in the region.

But then I moved to Poland.

One day, one of the girls that worked with me arrived at her shift, and I greeted her as usual.

Cheers Dominika, everything fine?

She said yes and asked how if everything was fine with me too. My answer was the standard: Everything great!

After my answer came another question. One that I couldn't answer because it was the first time someone asked it to me.

So why are you smiling? Some good news?

Following the surprise of hearing such inquiry, I just answered, "Oh, not really. But nothing bad happened either"

Since this day, I paid more attention to the facial expression of people around me. This led me to conclude that paying attention to this kind of physical and behavioral nuances is very helpful when adapting to a new country.

In Poland, people do not smile unless they have a reason to do so. A good reason to do so. The same characteristic I saw in other Slavic countries I visited. Slovakia, Serbia, Montenegro or Russia, just to name a few.

I am not saying that Slavs are always gloomy or cheerless. A joyful young couple talking during a walk or a dad playing with his daughter probably will laugh or even giggle. However, outside those moments, their facial expression is marked by seriousness.

What means to smile excessively in Slavic countries

People may misunderstand expressions of joy. To smile during a formal conversation can be seen as not taking it seriously. One time the grandma of my wife thought I was not believing her story just because I had a smile on my face.

In other situations, people can just think that you are a fool or have some psychological problem, as a Russian proverb says:

Smiling for no reason is a sign of stupidity.

But in South-America, you need a reason for not smiling

The same reflections I had in Poland may happen to Slavs when they hear the opposite in South-America.

Did something happen, Boris*? Why are you so serious?

*Yes, Boris is a very cliché Slavic name and I am happy to use it as an example.

If you adopt a Russian-style sober grimace in countries like Brazil or Colombia, there is a good chance you will confuse people. Some will think that you are deeply dissatisfied with life. Work colleagues will suppose that you are looking for a new job, and your mother-in-law will think you are feeling bad, or hungry.

Remember that most of the reasons for cultural shock happens in 4 different fields, and humor is one of them.

A last-advice, dear Slavs: it does not always mean flirting!

One misconception that some Europeans have in South-America is to confuse the polite smile given to strangers as hidden interests or even flirting. It is not flirting. Except, of course, if he or she also asks for your phone number and invite for a drink later. If this is the case and you accept, remember to smile back.

Questions to ask yourself:

To make your life easier, I prepared the template below. Seek the information about your new country in the ways I suggested previously *communities in social media and groups related to your interests) and complete it. At the end of the exercise, should be a plethora of information useful in your journey.

1st source of cultural shock: The Rules

How do people deal with regulations? Are they rigid and play strictly by the book or there is space to some negotiation? Are systems and procedures respected daily or used as guidelines, with frequent adaptations to daily circumstances? Are plans rigorously respected, or they are adjusted according to additional requests?

Your previous country:

Your new country:

2nd source of cultural shock: The Time

Do people arrive on time on every occasion, even informal ones? Is there some tolerance for delays? What happens when someone arrives 10 minutes late for a social gathering? How do we inform at work or university that something blocked the road, making it impossible to arrive on time? Is it normal to do over-hours or to extend a meeting beyond the scheduled time?

Your previous country:

Your new country:

3rd source of cultural shock: The Humor

Which level of formality is expected in a conversation at work or public office? Is it ok to do jokes as an icebreaker? Do people tend to laugh at small incidents or remain serious? Is a smile always considered a sign of joy or may be taken as disdain? Are puns and tricks common, or people tend to always behave seriously?

Your previous country:

Your new country:

4th source of cultural shock: The Communication

When it is time to take a decision, how is the communication process: direct and to the point, with no digressions, or it goes around many hypotheses and with space to different discussions? When people need to criticize a co-worker, do they use subtle language and avoid direct conflict, or they just say what they want to say without space for doubt? When people ask for a favor or a task, do they suggest indirectly using expressions like "maybe" or "would be nice if someone did that" or they straightforward tell you what they want? When someone needs to deny an invitation or a request, do they simply say "I can't do it, sorry" or they use excuses?

Your previous country:

Your new country::

RULE THREE - MAKE MEASURABLE GOALS AND STICK TO THEM

Remember at the beginning of the book when I wrote that some things explained here I learned by my own mistakes, and I don't want you to commit the same errors? This chapter exemplifies one of them. The rule here regards a mistake I committed in two of the three times I moved between countries.

To not have specific, measurable, achievable, realistic, and timely goals.

The first time I hit the road abroad was to live in the stunning city of Santiago, in Chile. I was inexperienced and going to work in a prestigious multinational company. They hired me with good expectations, and the beginning was quite positive. They even praised me for how fast I was learning both the job and Spanish. Things started to go sideways when I discovered Bellavista and Providencia, two of the bohemian districts of Santiago. And it got worse (or better, depending on the perspective) when they hired a new group of Brazilian trainees to whom I introduced the nightlife of the Chilean capital, their free club entrance for foreigners, free drinks for friendly Brazilians, free this and this...

If you are not aware of your responsibilities, those places will drag you out from Tuesday to Saturday. I was so dazzled with the party atmosphere of the city that I even decided to live at the side of my favorite pub, Flannery's.

That is when things got out of hand. Even receiving a better salary than in Brazil, I left Chile without saving virtually nothing.

Fortunately, I had a second chance. Actually, much better than just a second chance. I received an offer of the top player in my industry while I was still in Chile. Since there my own irresponsibility limited my career prospects, I took the chance it and moved.

My new job was in Doha, Qatar. Definitely a place where I would not be partying and having sleepless nights like I had in Santiago.

Before taking off to the Middle East, I made very specific goals to achieve. I researched the living costs and city prices, and realized that with a prudent lifestyle, in three years I would save money enough to leave and open my own business, or move to a calmer place. So, I planned to stay a maximum of three years there and keep as much as I could from my salary. Every month I was updating an Excel sheet to help me see how far I was from my goal, and how much I should save from my salary to achieve the amount I targeted.

Having those goals was a tremendous stimulus. I was a completely different man than the one that was enjoying rough nights in Chile and shaming himself by walking with a Gatorade bottle the next day. I was focused, punctual and disciplined not only at my work but also outside. To keep my fitness performance at the same level of my mental efforts, I also created physical and mental goals. I was hitting hard at the gym six times per week. While others were going for expensive happy hours, I resorted to stay home and use this time to exercise and learn a new idiom (which later proved useful to my next move[7]). Matteo, the Argentinian with whom I shared my apartment, said he couldn't believe someone would endure such strict targets and survive, that eventually I would break down. Matteo was wrong, I didn't break down.

They promoted me before completing two years in Qatar. Now, finally, I had some spare money to enjoy life, and I enjoyed it. I went to the brunches my colleagues were going and tasted again oysters and mai-tais. I also visited my girlfriend in Europe more frequently, and we traveled together.

Then another dilemma appeared: Life now was so satisfactory that it seduced me to stay more. Six months before completing three years, I achieved my initial financial target. Almost at the same time, I had an offer to move to Spain and work in a startup. I accepted, but it never went forward because of bureaucratic complications (which proved fortunate). Maybe it was a signal I should stay longer in Doha, saving money and eating seafood. But I decided to stick to my goals and left to Poland, the country of my girlfriend, and opened my business.

It was at this moment I committed my second mistake. I was very satisfied in achieving the professional, financial and physical goals I created before moving to Qatar. Therefore, just after the decision of moving to Poland, I made new targets. This time even more difficult.

Then I failed, and it took a while until realize that I overestimated my targets. I made them completely unachievable. Even if I was a local, those goals would be hard, but for a foreigner, they were unrealistic. I entered into despair and it took a while (and some financial losses) to put myself together and try again.

S.M.A.R.T

Having clear goals can be extremely useful and motivational. When I was melting under 48C in Doha waiting for a taxi or when a broken sewage pipe flooded my firm, my goals talked louder in my mind, saying something like:

Levi, we know it is unpleasant to have a pool of human excrement in the basement, but you are here for a reason, so put your boots, go down and check if a plumber is necessary.

When the situation is hard and you need to face big (or smelly) obstacles, your targets will push you to keep going.

Clear objectives are not useful only when you are in a difficult situation. They also will give a sense of orientation and help you to not get lost in epicurean party frenzies like those I had in Chile. If in Santiago I had a specific goal of what I wanted to achieve, instead of enjoy piscolas on a Wednesday, I would be sleeping earlier to be the best version of me in the next day. But I didn't have any measurable aim, except to enjoy life. And I am sorry, ladies and gentlemen, but be happy is not a goal. At least not a S.M.A.R.T one.

The dots between the letters are not an accident. S.M.A.R.T is an acronym to *Specific, Measurable, Achievable, Realistic, and Timely*. According to *MindTools*[8], the definition for each word is:

• **Specific**: Your goal should be clear and specific, otherwise you won't be able to focus your efforts or feel truly motivated to achieve it.

o Questions to ask: *What do I want to accomplish? Who is involved and where is it located?*

• **Measurable**: It is important to have measurable goals so you can track your progress and stay motivated. Assessing progress helps you to stay focused, meet your deadlines, and feel the excitement of getting closer to achieving your goal.

o Questions to ask: *How much or how many I want to accomplish? How will I know when it is accomplished?*

• **Achievable**: Your goal needs to be realistic and attainable to be successful. In other words, it should stretch your abilities but remain possible.

o Questions to ask: *How can I accomplish this goal? How realistic is the goal, based on other constraints, such as financial factors?*

• **Relevant**: This step is about ensuring that your goal matters to you, and that is also aligned with other relevant goals. We all need support and assistance in achieving our goals, but it is important to retain control over them. Thus, make sure your plans drive everyone forward, but that you're still responsible for achieving your own goal.

o The question to ask: *Does this seem worthwhile?*

• **Time-bound**: Every goal needs a target date so that you have a deadline to focus on and something to work towards. This part of the SMART goal criteria helps to prevent everyday tasks from taking priority over your longer-term goals.

o Questions to ask: *When I will achieve it? What should I start doing today?*

Now that you know how to define the targets to guide you in your new country and new life, I need to do two important disclaimers.

The first one is to do not make your goals the priority of your life. They should be significant tools to delineate your path and remember where you want to go, what you want to achieve. But still only tools. Therefore, when you define your plans, always execute them according to your principles. If you don't do a principle-centered approach to your goals, at some moment you may see yourself against your own code of conduct. And that is a conflict no man should look for. If your expat assignment demands you to go against what you believe, stick to your values. Just like my goals worked for me in Doha, your plan to reach your objectives should work for you and make you better, not oppose your ethical standards.

The second disclaimer is to make space for personal rewards. Break your goals in smaller steps and allow yourself to a treat when you reach them. It may sound Pavlovian, but this will motivate you to keep going and to face the next challenge. If possible, save a small part of your salary for the *joie de vivre*, the pleasant moments that even the most disciplined allow themselves to push the gloom away. Be it a cold one in the nearby beer garden, or a brunch with your friends, as you wish, but I assure you: It's worth it.

RULE FOUR - TALK WITH THE TAXI DRIVER AND TO THE GROCERY CASHIER

Imagine it is your first week in your new country. You are still not living in your permanent home, but staying in temporary accommodation until you finally decide what is the best part of the city for you.

Thus, you marked a meeting with a local real estate agent to see which kind of affordable and comfortable place is available in the region. Walking to the meeting, you stop to buy a sandwich in a convenience store and order a coffee to go. The young cashier is apparently learning her new job, so she asks you to be patient with a shy smile. After grabbing your cup, you enter the metro and sit at the side of a sympathetic woman in her 70s, and she asks what time is now. You answer her and grab your phone, to check in your social media if someone in the group of foreigners answered your question about what place is the best for a young man like you to live. When you arrive at your final station, you put your phone back in your pocket and realize that the elderly woman already left.

You walk a few miles more and finally arrive at the office, a few minutes in advance. While you are waiting at the reception, you sit on the left side of a dad with his toddler. The kid starts to play in your direction, so you smile and take your phone to finish reading whatever people wrote to your question in the group of foreigners. When it is time to start your meeting, the real estate agent, with the same smile of car salesmen and politicians, calls you to his office to show all the "incredible" opportunities you must see.

That is when you realized it was just another *expat trap*. And they are many. Nothing better than a foreigner looking, with urgency, for a house, car or insurance. Easy money for a good salesman, and there is a considerable chance he is not showing what is in your best interest, but rather the offers giving him the biggest commission. The nasty commonplace is that the worst options pay the best commissions to the seller, so the smiling sales representative has an extra motivation to push whatever garbage he has to some innocent expatriates.

I am not saying all professionals who boast titles like *advisor, agent, consultant, expert* and others are tricksters, but there might be a conflict of interests. So if you cannot trust them, who should you trust?

Some would go to the human resources department of their companies or to the student section of their universities to ask about their new country. Once in a while, there will be someone there to help, but often they will just be too busy in their tasks to assist you. After all, this is not their main function. Others will seek help from fellow foreigners, and that can be risky since many of those still will be in their *honeymoon* period with the new country (see chapter one), henceforth they will not know all the troubles to alert you.

So, who remains?

Where a foreign newcomer can find the ordinary expertise, the *savoir faire* and the wise advice about how everything around works?

The answer lies with our unsung heroes: the common folk! The young cashier with a shy smile at the convenience store. The elderly lady sat at your side and tried to talk to you about the weather. The dad whose toddler tried to play with you at the waiting line. What you were doing when those opportunities to have information about your new country appeared in front of you? You grabbed your phone to ask for advice of people that are not locals and may know less than you!

In any major city, you will have plenty of opportunities to ask your doubts to all those people around you in the cashier line or at the metro in a non-touristy area. Use those chances.

By talking to the common folk, those born and raised, you discover the real mishaps of the place and learn to survive the hustle and bustle. You will understand the atmosphere, learn how to avoid the trials and tribulations and master the needed street wisdom needed to skyrocket your adaptation. If you listen deeply to what others talk, you may even get the emotional nuances shaping the culture of your new home.

Pay attention to your surroundings instead of the black screen of your phone (although this may backfire, since maybe you are reading this book in it) and don't waste any chance to chitchat around. Not only you will learn about the out-of-the-way secrets of your new home, but also you may be invited to parties or discover a new culinary delight. I discovered kimchee in a casual conversation, and it became one of my favorites.

What are you waiting for then? Just talk to that lady in the metro about the possibility of raining today (and ask which transport is quicker if a storm happens).

RULE FIVE -DON'T LEAVE TO CALL TO YOUR PARENTS TOMORROW

If you are older than a teenager, there is a good chance you had one of those farewells from high-school, university or even from your group of friends from a previous job. You or someone else is moving out, so everyone meet and after a few drinks, comes the classical:

- *Now we do a pact! Let's promise to ourselves that this is not going to be our last meeting, guys! We will do it at least one time per year! Deal?*

And everyone agrees, of course.

Years come and years go, without those meetings happening again or only sporadically. After some time you start to lose contact with your old friends, including the ones that supported your career decisions or listened to your complaints about life. It's hard to deal with this disconnection, especially when you don't know anyone nearby. At some point, you think people forgot you.

Not everyone understands how different time zones or routines work, especially if they never lived far away. Maybe your friends' back home do not contact you because they think you are not available or interested. Don't take it personally. It is normal that while living abroad you need to be proactive to get in touch with people that stayed back home. When you get used to the idea that you also can call them, send greetings, ask how things are going or if the local team is doing fine, then you will realize they are still there and your old relationships are well-kept.

Fortunately, modern technology helps a lot to keep in touch, and there are some simple hints to help with your family and friends. One of my favorites is to use group chats in instant communicators like *WhatsApp*. For example, right now I am in a group of relatives, another of university friends, other of my former workmates from Qatar, another one from beer buddies in Warsaw, and finally a group of comrades from São Paulo. In this way, the group interactions get more dynamic and it is easier to organize get-togethers. A few of my friends visited me already in Europe, thanks to our conversations in *WhatsApp*.

But what about your parents?

In previous paragraphs, I wrote you should be proactive to get in touch with friends. This same statement takes a new dimension regarding family. Even if they respect your new routine and don't tell how much they are waiting for your call, parents will be jubilant when the phone rings and it is you. Your grandparents? The same (or maybe even more).

Most expats never ask themselves what are their parents' expectations about contact frequency or mode.

Have you asked that yourself?

Think about it. If you ask your grandmother or mother how frequently she would like to hear news from you, there is a good chance she will say something like "As much as possible!" The problem is, in another country - and drowned by new routines and efforts to adjust to the culture - you make this "as much as possible" much less than what was possible. By assigning the family contacts to a secondary place, we are not only depriving them of joyful moments, like when they see again the faces of daughters and grandsons, but also doing a disservice for our own adaptation efforts. As the specialist and expatriate Ana McGinley[9] wrote:

Relationships with family members are crucial in the preservation of self-identity in expat adults and children – especially when the culture of the host country is unfamiliar or confronting. Being able to 'be yourself' with the people who know you is a wonderful comfort often available in the company of family members.

It is vital to remember time doesn't stop when we move to another country, and it is difficult to deal with the beloved ones getting older. Mom and Dad will have some extra wrinkles and gray hair, but their smile when talking to you will always be the same.

If you have kids, they will grow up too and your parents will be heartbroken if they cannot see how their grandson is trying his first steps or their granddaughter performs during ballet class. For the kids, the contact with the rest of the family is a powerful bond to the familiar ties and an enriching experience. As the American writer Alex Haley once wrote: "Nobody can do for little children what grandparents do. Grandparents sort of sprinkle stardust over the lives of little children".

To deal with distance from family, the best way I found (thanks again to technology) is to use more videos, be it recorded or through video calls. When I moved abroad for the first time, this kind of resource still was not accessible and I felt guilty that I couldn't see my family enough, but things changed and now it is possible. I am not saying that everyone should do the same, but I try to see them via video calls at least three or four times per week.

It was not always like that. During my first years I was neglectful. As the common wisdom says, sometimes you learn about your mistakes in a hard way. Just when I moved from Qatar to Europe to start my business, I got immersed in the frenzy to have all prepared, solve all the bureaucratic paperwork, hire people and improve my language skills. One day I called my parents, and they told me they visited my grandmother. During the visit, grandma remembered me, asked how I was and said she would be very happy to talk to me. A few days later, I called again my parents, and they said multiple times that my grandma remembered me, so I arranged to call them in that afternoon when they would be at her house.

I called, my father answered, and I asked him if I could talk to grandma.

He gave the phone to her, and she asked "Hey, *meu fio*" (a tender way to refer to sons and grandsons). I tried to answer, but the quality of the call was terrible, so I told I would call later.

It was the day before Easter and I was supposed to travel to the city of my girlfriend to have dinner with her family. When I was there, I kept distracted by all the conversation and the banquet to the point I didn't check my phone. Just before sleep, I saw a message sent hours before by my dad, saying that my grandma was waiting for my call.

Oh no, I forgot to call! I texted back apologizing and told I would call her the next day, since it was too late in both places.

The next day, Easter morning, I woke up, took my phone and checked *WhatsApp*. There was a message from my dad there.

-    *Hey son, I have some hard news. Last night grandma felt bad. We rushed her to the hospital, but it was her time. She passed away.*

Do not delay the call to your parents (or grandparents) for tomorrow.

RULE SIX - DON'T LOOK BACK. THE HOME YOU LEFT DON'T EXIST ANYMORE

I remember clearly how was the last weekend before moving abroad. It was Carnival, and in Brazil it is celebrated everywhere, although in different manners. I was with a big group of friends in a small city where, during this time of the year, young students from different regions come to celebrate this annual party. We rented a house so during the day we drank beer, made barbecue and swam in the pool (which was tiny for all of us, but it was Carnival, so nobody cares). We gave pre-parties and went to the big celebrations during the night.

It was awesome, and it was supposed to be from Saturday to Tuesday. However, on Monday morning I received a call from the HR telling me that the bureaucratic procedures of my expatriation finished, so I should be flying to my new country next Wednesday. I needed to leave almost immediately to prepare my luggage.

Maybe because this was one of the last moments before I move out, I really missed Carnival during my first two years abroad. When I saw my friends enjoying it, while I was in places where this celebration is virtually nonexistent, it made me feel blue. After some time my pals also moved out, some of them married and had kids, and now, eight years later, I barely remind carnival exists. It is not important to me anymore.

I tell you this story to exemplify one thing: Few years after you move, the recognizable scenario you left behind will not be there anymore, or at least not as you had in your memory. This happens for two reasons: the first is that your home changed, the people and the places you used to go changed, and even the hobbies and popular trends changed. The second reason is that, after years out, you also change.

The most interesting thing is that you may not even be aware of the transformations you went through, just like when you lose (or gain) weight slowly and the people that notice are not the ones seeing you every day, but the aunt you visit once per year. As the Singaporean expat Bernie Low wrote at the *GaijinPot Blog*[10]:

Each time I went back to Singapore I would be excited to return to where I had grown up, nostalgia tugging at my heart strings each time I heard the roar of an airplane engine – I was going home! But what happens when home is no longer home? When instead of warmth and nostalgia all you feel is displacement and loss? [...] I feel like a foreigner in my own country. There is an echoing bitter aftertaste that

I cannot quite identify at the end of each day. I am living there, but each time it grows ever more distant, like the best friend you used to have that you're drifting apart from and it frightens me.

Some minor differences in your accent will make people laugh. Other differences, like the changes in your personality or habits, will be noticed by your friends or relatives, and their approaches may vary. Some will see those changes as matureness developing after facing difficulties across the world. Others, however, may understand it as pretentious or even fake, made just to impress. Digression: in some cases, they are right, since I saw a fair quota of expats that artificially change their accent and pretend to appear cosmopolitan, but just look ridiculous.

The two transformations, the one back in our land and the other inside ourselves, result in one thing: the home you left behind is not there anymore. It still exists and probably is very familiar to you, but it is not the same. People there are not the same, neither you. Some expats don't realize this and frequently consider going back just because they deeply miss their home. My answer is always the same:

Which home do you miss: the one you keep in your memories or the one that is real now?

If it is the second case, it is understandable. I also miss the place where my family lives and where I spent my childhood. On the other hand, if what you miss are your memories, you must be aware they are just that: memories. To reproduce, or even worse, re-enact memories is not a goal that typically leads to a meaningful life.

But how to deal with this? How to deal with this urge, created in difficult moments, that you should throw everything in the air and go back to the place where you feel safe?

The first step is to understand this urge is natural. The same proverb about the greener grass of the neighbor applies here. When difficulties appear in your new country and you think about how would be better if you never left in the first place, remember that you also have no idea how things would be if you were still living there. Time flows and our age is far from stable. Besides, remember your targets, your goals and the reason you moved out in the first place. Chapter 4, rule three, remember?

If there is one trick tremendously helpful and which I recommend is to set yourself a minimum time, at least three to six months, where you don't allow yourself to think about moving back. During this time, remove any conjecture about how life would be if you were still there or what you would be doing at your previous job. Instead, spend your mental energy learning to love just where you are, and how this new environment can support your goals, and this thought will keep you going.

RULE 7 - DON'T LOOK FOR THE SAME. STICK TO WHAT IS SIMILAR

Almost everyone has a few family practices perpetuated from infancy to adulthood, which are eventually called *house traditions*. Mine was the family barbecue. One or two times per month my father turned on the *churrasqueira* (an intimidating word basically meaning "grill") around noon, my mom prepared *vinagrete*, and one or two hours later all of us served ourselves from thin stripes of *picanha, alcatra* and all sorts of typical Brazilian cuts, together with bread rolls filled with *vinagrete*. Just by writing this paragraph, I feel the craving for it, something difficult to anyone foreign to my region to understand.

Outside my country is nearly impossible to find the same kind of cuisine, except in places where you have a big Brazilian community or demand for different types of meat. Qatar was in the second case. Two restaurants served those cuts there for rich sheiks willing to taste it. I was not a frequent client of those since I was not willing to pay multiple times more than what I was used to. Thus, there was me, in the middle of the desert, deeply craving the meat and the moments I had during my whole life. That is when I realized I lived with two Argentinians. They knew some restaurants where the price tag was not high, and the best: we had company discounts!

Although Argentinian cuts differ greatly from the Brazilians, the environment and the taste was still fine. Albeit there was no *vinagrete*, there was another remarkably tasty sauce: *chimichurri*. Then I saw it was possible to satiate my appetite without emptying my pockets. I also found in supermarket cuts similar to *alcatra* and prepared it at home. To complete my weekend replicas of childhood rituals, I used to call my parents during those times and have long talks where we updated each other about our lives.

Though I didn't have my parents present there (as well our typical bread rolls called *pão francês*, which were impossible to find), the weekends with *churrasco*-imitation were enough to catapult my mood and make me filled with satisfaction, happiness, and protein.

I told you this story because, if you are already living abroad, probably you met other foreigners constantly complaining about how much they miss what they had back home. Maybe you even are one of them (no offense intended). Food and culinary ingredients are the most common reason for ranting. Looking for an *expat products* store is valuable when adapting to life in a new country. Usually, those stores will have the most famous food items from selected countries, like condiments, beverages, sweets or ingredients. It is especially convenient for anyone with kids going through adaptation.

Besides food, this dissatisfaction can build up from many other items that are inaccessible abroad. Things like hobbies, sports, climate, your favorite place, drinks and routines. The affliction takes many forms. For example, an article of *Worklife*[11] described the case of Joe Watson. He relocated to Hong Kong from Atlanta for six years and not being able to watch his sports teams on TV made him yearn for life back home. The consultancy firm *Expatica*[12][12] exemplified this problem, and the opportunities derived from it:

When you're not in your hometown, you need to adapt to what's available in your new environment. For instance, you may have only ordered coffee from a particular company, but you may have to adjust to whatever type of coffee you can get in your locality. Weird smells? You must just get used to it. Constantly complaining about how you can't find the same brands as in your country or that you prefer the public transportation network back home doesn't build a healthy relationship with your new place of residence Try to focus on the positives and venture outside your comfort zone. Maybe you'll find an even better brand of coffee in the process.

The paragraph above describes a pattern I saw among many expats all over the world. A common behavior which I will call here the *analogous to nothing syndrome* (ANS). It happens when, longing for something they had before and now it inaccessible in a foreign country, the person completely loses the capacity to substitute his previous desire for something similar. As if that dish, hobby, or Wednesday night event was *analogous to nothing,* an exclusivity only his beloved country had and there is nothing in the universe to substitute it.

Sometimes the *analogous to nothing syndrome* comes from the pride of what we judge as typical, traditional, or just very cool in our country. Like a Chilean expatriate in France misses drinking *Piscolas* because of the impossibility to find Pisco (a Chilean-Peruvian national drink) and don't realize he can instead use Grappa with a similar result. Or a Californian casual-surfer living in Austria, frustrated with the lack of waves (and sea at all) but not realizing how satisfying could be to snowboard in the challenging slopes of Tyrol.

On other occasions, the ANS results from a lack of creativity or knowledge. To exemplify it, I ask your permission to tell another personal story. During my first winter in Europe, more or less around January, I was feeling tired and demotivated, since it was dark almost all the time. I was also getting sick frequently, and then I realized this was a message from my body. It was almost shouting to me "Hey, there is something wrong! I need sunlight!". My skin color changed from the usual olive tone to a pale shade. I went to the doctor, and he asked for some exams. When the results came, we understood everything:

Severe lack of vitamin D.

There's a good reason vitamin D is also known as "the sunshine vitamin". The nutritionist Ryan Raman[13][14] explained that *When your skin is exposed to sunlight, it makes vitamin D from cholesterol. The sun's ultraviolet B (UVB) rays hit cholesterol in the skin cells, providing the energy for vitamin D synthesis to occur.* Since my genetics provided me with a darker color, ideal for places with strong sunshine like Brazil, it was *over filtering* the scarce sunlight of the central European winter.

Here we had a problem. I *couldn't* bring the Brazilian sunshine to here, and at this point holidays were out of the question. So I needed a bit of creativity and some technology to solve the issue. The solution after all is to take vitamin tablets every morning, and an artificial light imitating the sun. The physiological problems faded and my humor, mood and productivity had a boost.

What this proved is that even the tropical sunshine is not *analogous to nothing* and can be substituted by something similar if you need it. Eventually, the search for a similar thing can even unveil other opportunities. Mark Callaghan, a British that moved to the USA and was badly craving for his typical "Sunday lunch swimming with gravy", had his story told by *Worklife*[14]4:

"He did something most homesick expats don't do — he turned his longing for home into a successful livelihood, later launching British Corner Shop, an online supermarket delivering British groceries worldwide, primarily to expats wanting a taste of home."

It is likely that, freeing yourself from the inertia and frustration caused by not finding the *same* you had before, you will find something *similar*. If you are a Russian in the USA, maybe you miss celebrating Orthodox Easter. In the case your city doesn't have many of your countrymen, use your creativity and you might find Serbians, Romanians and many other nationalities that share traditions and prepare a delicious *kulich*.

The same is valid for routines. I remember that during my time in the Middle East, there was a group of *jogging* expats. A lot of them were Australians, North Americans and Europeans. People from places where jogging is a good way to exercise outdoors and socialize. But outdoor exercising in Doha, where summer temperatures could reach 50 degrees Celsius, could be a health risk to those daring to do a physical activity outside.

So how those people were *jogging*?

I read more about this group and realized that they were not jogging indoors, but rather in shopping malls, multipurpose centers and other acclimatized environments. The association became so popular that the hotel Hyatt Plaza sponsored a similar initiative in the city[13][14][15].

Jogging in a shopping mall. This is what I call *creativity*! It is certainly not the same as what they had in their countries, but it is similar and as the success of the group showed, it was also fun.

This *similar* you will find may become your new standard, who knows? I would never expect that one day I would be more interested in watching winter sports than a carnival parade. As those examples prove, the sunshine of the tropics, the mild weather of the Mediterranean, the exotic cuisines, the pacific waves or the biggest party on the planet are not unreplaceable by something analogous. So why would you think the thing you are missing is *analogous to nothing*?

Just look, in your new country, for something comparable to what you had before and embrace it. Instead of look for the same, stick to what is similar, and enjoy it.

RULE 8 – ADAPT TO THE LOCAL ETIQUETTE, BUT ALLOW YOURSELF MINOR CONCESSIONS

At the beginning of this book, I wrote that the instructions proposed here are universal, not restricted to one single area of the globe. However, some rules may apply in more distinct ways than others depending on what is the difference between your current and previous country. This is especially true for the rule of this chapter: Adapt and respect the local etiquette but allow yourself minor concessions.

If you, dear reader, moved out from Canada to the USA or from Scotland to England, maybe you will see my next paragraphs and think "Oh Bollocks! My adjustment to the local way of life was so smooth, why such a drama?". Well, the adaptation at my first move, from Brazil to Chile, was also not difficult. The few obstacles were only internal (missing family, friends and all other things from home) because the externals like language or customs were not very different from what I had before. That is because Chileans are not that different from Southeastern-Brazilians, as much as residents from Toronto are not that different from New Yorkers.

On the other hand, if you are moving to a country with distinctive courtesy code, formalities and behavior conventions, you may find yourself lost. Without even noticing, you might gain a poor reputation or enter a fight. My whole life I crossed my legs when sitting for longer times. For me, it was just an insignificant gesture done to feel comfortable. I thought that until I move to the Middle East.

In one of my first days in Doha, while I was in the HR department waiting for some bureaucratic procedure, I crossed my right leg over the left, leaving it parallel to the floor and with the sole of my shoe visible to everyone at my left. After a few seconds, a man around his 50s, dressing a typical *thawb*, told something in Arabic to me in an unpleasant tone. I realized I made something wrong and later understood that showing the sole of your shoes to someone there is an insult. So, if you are reading this, middle-aged stranger in a white *thawb*, I am sorry for showing you my shoe's sole.

There are two great ways to fire up your understanding of the local etiquette. The first one is also the easiest:

Watch other people!

The quickest way to adapt to other cultures is to watch the

locals. Do not be cocky and realize that the meaning of certain traditions may be inaccessible to new joiners, particularly if you don't know the idiom or *ethos* of the place. Rachel Heller, the author of the page *Rachel Ruminations*, wrote an interesting story about her time as an American in the Netherlands[15][16]:

> *Sometimes the biggest differences are the smallest. It took me a couple of months before I realized that, rather than just placing a plateful of cookies on the table in front of visitors when we sat down to drink tea, I had to explicitly offer the cookies to them. They wouldn't help themselves to cookies without being offered. I thought they just didn't want any. And I had to offer them a second cup of tea, rather than expecting them to take it. I sat there, eating cookies and refilling my own tea, and didn't realize how incredibly impolite I was being! So watch their behavior carefully: notice how they shake hands, how they sit, how they handle food, and so on.*

Maybe Rachel could see in the guest's faces that they were not serving themselves because she was not doing what the local etiquette tells in the Netherlands (explicitly offer it to the guests). When you live outside your country, it can be challenging to interpret facial expressions.

The research of the American psychologists Hillary Anger Elfenbein & Nalini Ambady[17][18] concluded that we recognize facial emotions better when observing people similar to us in terms of nationality and ethnic group. Therefore, if you are in an unfamiliar environment, with conspicuous differences to your homeland, maybe observing people will not tell much to you. Therefore, as Rachel Heller advises, just ask people what are the local rules of politeness.

The second great way to assimilate the local etiquette is more demanding, but (at least for me), very rewarding:

Learn the local language, or at least try.

To learn the idiom of your new country will open a whole new world to you. Not only you will be able to say things like *Thank you* or *Please* when shopping at the grocery store or ordering in a café, but you will take the nuances that shape people's mood in their daily activities. To understand the local jokes and insults will give you a great idea of what is funny and what is outrageous in your new home.

The cognitive scientist Lera Boroditsky in her research affirmed that the language shapes the way we think[18,19]. Therefore, by learning the local language, you will be able to think like a local, and that escalates your chances of success (or at least survival) in your new environment. Which incentive can be better than this? As the Austrian philosopher Ludwig Wittgenstein wrote[19], *"The limits of my language mean the limits of my world"*.

While I recommend you adapt to the local politeness standards, especially in public, it would be delusional to expect that someone simply change his whole behavior just because he/she is moving abroad. The good news is: you don't need to.

There are always plenty of concessions you can allow yourself without being rude. I am used to eating pizza with a fork and knife, something common in my region since the pizza dough there is quite thin, so grabbing it can make a mess. Neither in Qatar nor Poland people eat in that way, but still, all the time when I go to a pizzeria I ask for a fork and a knife. Some people look to me and some probably think that this is weird. However, the comfort of eating pizza *in my way* outweighs any discomfort from people looking to me and asking themselves "why this guy is doing this?". It is not impolite, but just weird. And it is not rude to be slightly weird.

The more you adjust to the local customs, the more people will *allow* you to be peculiar. It is almost like there is an *expat behavioral* bank account. If you adopt a posture of inflexibility, always answering invitations to traditional dishes with "No, I am not used to that", or replying questions about local matters with "I am not interested in it", the balance of your *behavioral bank account* with people around will be empty. When that happens, even minor signals, like your clothes, may send a message you don't want to integrate, and people will just give up.

However, if your colleagues or spouse's family see that you are trying to learn the basics of their language, appreciating their dishes and drinks and even commenting on the local sports news, they will not mind your eccentricities. When I am watching TV, sometimes I like to sit in a lotus position (maybe I am revealing too much in this book, sorry). My wife told me it was weird, but since I was watching their favorite sport and trying to talk in their language, they just were ok with it and thought it was some typical way of Brazilians to sit (it is not).

That is part of the beauty of being a foreigner: others often will think that whatever oddness you have is just a typical thing of your country, and you will not look so odd.

So aim to adjust to the local etiquette, but allow yourself minor concessions.

RULE 9 – DON'T TAKE THINGS FOR GRANTED: MAKE A PROPER PLAN B

The time to repair the roof is when the sun is shining.

John F. Kennedy, former U.S. President.

It is uncommon to board a plane to start a new life focusing on unexpected and unpleasant situations. Still, you prepare yourself for the difficulties you judge possible, like not passing the probation time of your new employer or not being approved at university. As much as my experience shows me, expats are usually well prepared for the problems arising at the beginning of their life abroad.

Nonetheless, time passes and you get more settled, more comfortable with your surrounding and take things for granted. That is why this rule is among the last in this book. It is more useful to those already living as expats for some time.

The surprises that can storm your life greatly differs among countries. If you are living in the Middle East, you may get locked in civil unrest or geopolitical disputes. In South America, a hyper-inflation cycle can destroy the power of purchase and make your salary worth much less than what you had before moving out. In the USA, if you are in an accident not covered by your insurance, a medical bill might drain all your savings. In the seismic region knows as *the Pacific Ring*[2020], lives can change completely during earthquakes or tsunamis (like the one of 2004 in Indonesia or 2011 in Japan).

Even when there is no geopolitical crisis or natural cataclysms around, there are still the typical corporate problems that, in some locations, have a different dimension. In places like the United Arab Emirates or Qatar, if you lose your job, you may have only one month to leave the country. In Singapore, it can be even worse, with a deadline of only two weeks to get out. When I lived in Doha, it was common to see used luxury cars sold with huge discounts when an oil company laid off personnel. This is because their former staff had little time to pack the luggage and leave. Therefore, to sell their vehicles, even at a smaller price, was already a victory. That was the reason so many people there preferred to rent a car instead of buying one.

When we start a new life abroad, sometimes we ignore the chances it might not go as expected. We want to keep our morale, confidence and spirit. We want to believe that it is going to be a glorious year. This wishfulness increases if we didn't witness any recent major problem, and our perception that nothing bad is going to happen inflates. It is the *survivorship bias* the Nobel Prize winner Daniel Kahneman explained so well in his book *Thinking. Fast and Slow*[21].

Don't get me wrong here. It is essential to have a positive mindset, hope and work for the best outcome otherwise, you would never board the plane to move abroad. However, it is equally crucial to analyze the risks (even the rare ones) and find out possible alternatives.

Bottom line: The chances of happening an unlikely surprise increase across the years, and eventually the implausible event will knock at your door. So have a Plan B! And maybe even a C.

The best way to start a Plan B is to know as much as you can your failure risks. This is possible only talking to people that experienced failure. I recognize it is difficult to make others disclose their misfortunes, but it is worth to try. The next step is to compile all the possible situations representing a hazard and work in their contingency. For this, you can also use the experience of other foreigners by asking them in social media, expat meetings and blogs. Which kind of failures can happen? What they did to protect themselves? How they reacted when the event arose? How they prepare for it now?

For natural cataclysms there are well-known standard procedures. In Japan, for example, there are earthquake emergency packs with water, canned food, blankets, etc. In Indonesia, after the tsunami, they build shelters in the most exposed beaches and hotels prepare evacuation protocols with antecedence.

While I would not recommend to cool down and take a breath if a hurricane or tsunami is approaching, with a crisis of sociopolitical nature is different. For this kind of situation, it may be better to sit back, think and not rush to make decisions. A good example is the tumultuous relation between North and South Korea, which at every threat scares some expats but nothing serious happened in the last decades. A similar situation happened in Armenia in 2018, when major protests erupted in their capital, Yerevan. The city stopped and was relatively chaotic for a few days. I was there spending holidays, and even before I came back, everything already went back to normal. Of course, civil unrest may turn into a long crisis and, sometimes, even wars. But surely most of them don't go that far and should not be a reason for panic.

Putting aside natural and sociopolitical reasons, another risk is more individual-related. In countries where there is a short time-frame to leave in case of losing a job or student status, it is important to ask to rent agreements include a termination clause. This would make you exempt of any fines to the landlord in the case they terminate your job against your will. In most places nowadays there is also a variety of job loss insurances covering these situations.

As a personal advice, one thing that always worked very well for me is to live *light*, in the sense of not accumulate long contracts, obligations, or assets. While for a big family this may be challenging, for singles or young couples it is a great alternative. During my time in Chile, I never bought a car and the contract with my company assured me that if they dismissed me, they would cover any fine of my rent agreement. It was not the case in Qatar, but since I was sharing my flat there, after resigning from my job I just needed to find a substitute to occupy my room. I also didn't need to sell any car because my flatmate Matteo had a nice deal with me, where I paid for his fuel, so he took me to and from work. Another very helpful strategy was to always rent furnished apartments, so I didn't need to buy and sell furniture or worse, move it from one country to another.

It was good that I was living *light* since my last move was not smooth. I needed to use my Plan B, and the reason for it is not any described before. Therefore, I ask again for your patience for a small personal story, and I promise it can be useful for you.

Remember that at the beginning of this book I wrote that in Qatar I had clear professional and financial targets, and after reaching them I planned to leave? So yes, after achieving my desired promotion and saved money enough for my projects, I planned to live in a different environment, and out of the big-corporation world. I looked for a job and one startup in Barcelona took my attention. We exchanged some emails, made an interview via Skype, and they asked me to visit their Spanish headquarters. There I talked to the CEO and solved some of these modern challenges startups apply during their selections. Few days and a call later, I got the job.

Simultaneously, I also had a job offer from a huge e-commerce corporation in Poland. Even though Poland was an interesting country to live (my girlfriend was Polish), I didn't want to move from one big corp to another, so I refused their job and accepted the Spanish offer. A few days later, I gave my one-month notice period in Doha.

Only two weeks before I finally leave for Spain, they called me and told me they didn't have the resources needed to apply for my visa. They told me I should do it myself, by my own resources and taking the risk of losing anything that I invested if the visa was rejected.

I knew that changing my life and depending on the bureaucratic skills of a small startup (where the CEO interviewed me with a greasy NASA t-shirt) was risky. So even before I had their job offer, I was also working on my Plan B: to open my own business.

To be specific, I started working on a backup plan one year before, doing market research to decide which cities were the most attractive in Poland and contacting business owners wanting to sell their enterprises. Some of them answered me positively. Therefore, when the NASA-Shirt CEO of the Spanish startup called me and gave me the bad news of their lack of structure, I jumped into the plan B. Immediately I made an offer to acquire a Polish business from a couple that wanted to live in a calmer place after their first baby.

However, a few months later this plan also broke down. After I move to Poland and just before I transfer them the money, they gave up selling the business. So, I went for plan C: Open my own company from zero.

After all those years, the company is still working, so even a plan C can endure if executed consciously. On a side note, the move to Poland instead of Spain gave me other surprises, but this time they were very positive.

At the end of the day, the most important to remember is simple: do not think improbable and unpleasant situations *will never* happen to you. Be prepared. After all, this may turn into a greater opportunity, as I will explain in the last chapter.

RULE 10 – GET OVER THE FACT THAT YOU WILL NEVER BE 100% NATIVE
(And you don't need to)

I start this chapter making a small excuse: the title you see above is not completely true. There are exceptions, subordinate to specific contexts, where expats become *like a native*. For example, in the French south-west, where some long-term Brits living among wineries abandoned their *fish and chips* and become more French than the locals, as the blog *Bordeaux Expats* reported[21][22]:

58-year-old Darren Taylor moved to the Dordogne from Essex 30 years ago because of his love of the novels of Proust and the poetry of Arthur Rimbaud, which he used to borrow from Dagenham Library.

He said: "You'll have to excuse me, it's such a long time since I spoke English. What's happening over there now anyway? Is Sven still England manager? Is Minder still on? I wouldn't know. I spend my days listening to the music of George Brassens and sipping pastis."

Pensioner Norman Kemp said, "Don't be deceived by my prominent bulldog tattoos. That was the old me. Nowadays whenever I'm not preparing magret de canard aux pommes sarladaises, I'm practicing the accordion or playing pétanque in the village square in my favourite beret.

It is refreshing to see cases like the above mentioned, where immigrants adapt so flawlessly. However, two points make these exceptions. The first is the context: The United Kingdom and France are neighbors with centuries of cultural, social, and economical entanglement. Therefore, the civilizational difference is reduced by mutual influences and the expat adjustment is quicker. The second point is that even in the British-in-France context there are plentiful examples of not-so-smooth adaptation, to the point of existing a mutual-help social network. The name of it is "Survive France".[22][23].

Therefore, this chapter is especially for those moved (or planning to) between countries not that similar. And if you arrived until here in this book, congratulations: you already know how to go through the worst phases of your new life. The German firm Archer Relocation designed the *Expat Adjustment Curve,* where the first stages are slightly similar to the phases described in the opening of this book, but with a different end:

1. *Honeymoon Phase*
2. *Initial Culture Shock*
3. *Superficial Adjustment*

4. *Culture Shock*

5. *Recovery*

6. *Integration*

The fundamental difference here is the sixth phase. Who reaches the Integration overcame the culture shock (our previous chapters help you with it) and recovered to run the show in their new life. As much as achieve this stage of adaptation is a brilliant victory, there are different levels of it. We can break down the concept of integration in 4 different types:

• Economic Integration – It is when foreigners work and generate wealth for themselves via their salaries and profits, and to their new country by paying taxes. They add their contribution both as supply, by their products, and demand, by their consumption. Skilled expats usually achieve this type quickly, but for students or non-working spouses it can take longer.

• Social – When people mingle with the locals, adopt social codes of the new country and its etiquette. Although the personal efforts to achieve social integration are important, how fast you will achieve depends also on how friendly is the population. The portal *Internations* made a research[23][24] about a similar subject and concluded that in places like Mexico, Costa Rica, Ecuador or Colombia, to create a social circle can be much easier than in Nordic countries or Saudi Arabia.

• Cultural – This kind of integration is when people adopt the habits and culture of the new place. To reach a full cultural integration, it is indispensable to have a good understanding of the local language and go across all its components (music, literature, beliefs and celebrations). The cultural integration can be even harder than the social integration if your original country and the new one are from different civilizational foundations, for example, India and Eastern Europe.

- Emotional – This is the last type of integration in the list for a reason: it is the hardest. I may take longer to explain emotional integration because it is essential for understanding this whole chapter. There is a word in my native language called *saudade* that is considered almost untranslatable but fits very well in this description. We may define *saudade* as the presence of absence, the yearning for something or someone that right now is unreachable, and whose absence creates a void in your inner self. It is not only missing, and does not have a completely negative meaning because it brings sadness and joy together. It is, as translated by older generations, *the love remains.* We can translate a partial emotional integration as loving your new country and shaping your personality by its influences. On the other hand, the fully integrated will go beyond and not feel *saudade* from his origins.

If you are already living abroad for some time, you probably are thinking how far you are in those four different dimensions. The good news is, as stated in the title of this chapter, you don't need to achieve all of them. In Chile, I was very well-integrated economically, socially, and culturally. I didn't need to do much effort since they are relatively close to Brazil in all those components. This similarity plays a big role. That is why in Poland, to reach the same level of assimilation from Chile it took much longer. In Qatar, I achieved economic integration but the social and cultural aspects were distant from my daily life.

What about emotional integration? Even though I had part of my personality changed by every country that I lived in, my core is still the same, and it is Brazilian. Therefore, differently than the British mentioned at the beginning of this chapter, I was never 100% emotionally integrated, and probably I will never be. I will always feel *saudade* of the southeastern plains of Brazil.

And this is ok.

It is almost the rule when you are a first-generation immigrant.

In an article of *Humanity in Action Denmark*, I read two stories that exemplify it. One from Savas Coskun and the other from Sabeena Din, who moved, respectively, from Turkey and Pakistan to Denmark[24][25].

It was the experience of travelling back and living one year in Turkey that convinced Coskun that whatever cultural identity meant; he had to have a mixture of both cultures in his identity. "Until ten years ago I said I was Turkish only," he says, "because saying to say I was Danish seemed a little false to me. And then I went to Turkey for a year and realized that I cannot be just Turkish. I have to be Turkish-Danish. I have to be both. Like Coskun, Sabeena Din, a 21-year-old born in Denmark, has two identities. When she is in Denmark, she feels more Pakistani. When she goes to visit Pakistan, she feels more Danish. However, Din does not feel that it is a crisis for her. "It is not a bad thing".

To make the best efforts to integrate into a new country is not only good for you. If you plan or already have children, this will have an enormous positive impact on them. Descendants of first-generation, well-assimilated immigrants and growing up in the company of native children will carry the advantage of youth years that significantly change them in comparison to their parents. This will allow them to adjust (economically, culturally, socially and emotionally) to a considerably greater degree.

Even doing your best efforts, still there is a good chance you will never be like a native (especially if you are a first-generation newcomer like me). Even after learning the language, you still will have an accent that will persist during decades. You will still have your tastes for food, music and traces in your personality shaped in your fatherland. If you are moving to a country racially homogeneous like some in Asia or Eastern Europe, you will also be the person looking different.

I have some great news for you: all those things can turn into opportunities. Your varied taste for food and music can give way to very interesting conversation topics. Your accent and knowledge of a foreign language can be useful to understand the so common loanwords from a globalized world. Those holidays you celebrated back in your country can double the opportunities for fun. With my wife we celebrate both Valentine's (14 of February) as her tradition and *Dia dos Namorados* (12 of June) as mine, so we have twice the amount of romantic dinners than a standard couple!

Equally, the matter of having a different skin color or ethnicity nowadays can open doors to great opportunities. In Poland, it is normal that younger people come talking to me in English, since I look like a foreigner, and when I answer in their language, I hear nice compliments and salutations for learning their idiom. The same would be if a westerner moved to Thailand and mastered Thai. In homogeneous countries, with a quick look people will know you are a foreigner and while this may scary some expats, it is a great chance to surprise and earn the local admiration.

Nobody likes the arrogant and pretentious expat that prefers to show off his differences at every point while despising the social and cultural features of his new home. But the complete opposite, the expat wishing to cut his roots and be like a local in every aspect, risk to enter a road to frustration due to unachievable goals.

You don't need to lose your roots to be the guy from a snowless country talking about winter sports with his Norwegian workmates, or the American that moved to South-Africa and now invite his neighbors for a *braai* (South African barbecue). In countries where people expect you to be just *another foreigner* that they have no interests in common, you will be in high-regard if you go beyond their expectations.

CONCLUSION: ALLOW YOURSELF TO GET LOST ONCE IN A WHILE

Arriving at the final words of this book, one thing must be said: to read until here you are already made a step towards a positive life overseas, but I hope it is not the last. After eight years of living abroad, a lot changed since my first year in Santiago. Countries and continents changed, but I am still learning how to be the best version of an *expat*, the best possible neighbor, teammate, co-worker, and husband. I hope you also found points in your expat journey that can improve. Be it calling to your parents more frequently, chat with the taxi driver, overcoming the cultural shock or understanding what are your goals and what you are looking for.

This learning must not cease, and the frustration should be kept away by leveling what we expect to our current conditions. If you want to raise your targets, be aware you also must raise your capacity, which is done by learning. As a matter of fact, flawed expectations are one of the main reasons so many foreigners are frustrated in their assignments abroad. Including me sometimes. I can list some cases:

What was expected: *The living cost there is really low, so I will save a considerable share of my salary!*

What is in reality: The costs can be expensive in the beginning. It is common to overcompensate in superfluous things like touristic restaurants while adapting to the new life. But sooner or later you will find the good and inexpensive local *trattoria*.

What was expected: *My social life will thrive with new friends from all over the world, just like during my student exchange in Europe!*

What is in reality: Adults have obligations like family and work. People may decline invitations and social gatherings can be scarce. Eventually, you will find your group and enjoy some drinks (and they will not be the cheap ones of the student years).

What was expected: *I love learning new languages! I already bought some audiobooks, so when I arrive I can already go conversational!*

What was in reality: It takes time to be colloquial, but one day you will get the joke, laugh and the others around will get surprised that now they cannot talk about you without you understanding them.

What was expected: *I will not change my diet too much. In* *those global days, I can find all the food I want everywhere I go.*

What was in reality: That kind of fruit you used to pay 1 dollar per kg in your hometown now costs 5 and even doesn't look good. However, there is this local alternative, and even though you never saw it before, you taste it and discover how delectable can be your new place.

Those are only some examples I saw and lived. Maybe you know others.

The fact is that in our complex world, expectations tend to deviate from reality. This is not necessarily negative. Frequently they are profoundly positive for us. Some years ago, an expat rushing to go to an important meeting took the wrong way in public transport and went to the middle of nowhere. It was his first day in his new country, and he was completely lost. Besides, nobody there spoke any language he could understand.

Until a girl appears and offers him help to go back to the city.

He married that girl later. And now he is thanking you for reading his book.

APPENDIX - APPS AND TOOLS FOR THOSE MOVING OR LIVING ABROAD

To find a place to live: Some expats try to choose a place to live before arriving in their new country. To sign any contract based on pictures or videos can be unnecessarily risky and lead to disappointment. The best way to solve this problem is to rent a stress-free accommodation on a website like Airbnb while in your first weeks you visit your selected properties and choose properly. The advantage of Airbnb over other accommodation websites like Booking.com and Expedia is that frequently there are discounts for stays longer than a week.

To try it, download Airbnb by this link and win a $36 discount (or equivalent) in your first reservation. https://www.airbnb.com/c/jonataslevib?currency=USD

To learn the language and the culture: Some people are used to language apps like Duolingo. I am passionate about Lingq because of its extremely friendly interface, the community of users where everyone helps each other correcting exercises, the possibility of import books, articles and songs to the app. You can use it to learn a new idiom and immerse in its culture at the same time. Using it I reached a conversational level in one of the hardest European languages, Polish, without going to any formal course.

You can check Lingq by visiting: http://bit.ly/36qzd6n

To transfer money between your old and new country: This recommendation saved me once, when just after arrival I realized I miscalculated the amount of money to bring. To do a normal international transfer would mean losing with bad exchange rates. Transferwise has rates much better than most banks and their transfers may take less than 24 hours.

Create your account using this link and win $20 in your first transfer: http://bit.ly/2TVU0vZ

To not confuse currencies or overspend: XE currency converter is both a website and a mobile app easy to use and updated in real-time. Available at: https://www.xe.com/currencyconverter/

To find a quick loo, anywhere: It will take a while until you know where are the public bathrooms in your new place. Meanwhile, you can use Flush, an app available to Android and Apple mobiles with a database of tens of thousands of public toilets ready for fast and offline access. Download it at Google Play Store in http://bit.ly/2TRhUIZ (available also at Apple Store).

To compare the cost of living: There are two websites, each with millions of prices in their databases, are essential to estimate if your salary will be enough to make the ends meet. They are Numbeo (https://www.numbeo.com/) and Expatistan (https://www.expatistan.com/)

To rent your former house or apartment and make some extra: I already recommended Airbnb before, but this time is for a different purpose. When we move out not completely sure if we will come back, or have no time to find a tenant or sell our property, a good solution can be to make it available at Airbnb for short-term rental. They even have tools to manage the property remotely and handle things like cleaning and insurance. It is not rare that people make twice the amount of cash on Airbnb compared to what they would earn if they simply rented it for a single tenant.

You can check the option of becoming an Airbnb Host through this link (where you will also earn $10): http://bit.ly/36mBNKB

To be updated about the most cutting-edge tips and tricks for expats and long-term travelers: The blog of my consultancy firm, where I share weekly insights of life overseas. https://expatriateconsultancy.com/digital-nomads-expats-and-travellers-blog/
and my Facebook page: www.facebook.com/leviporai

DID YOU ENJOY THIS BOOK?

The best award I could have is your opinion! I would be glad to read your thoughts in a review in Goodreads and Amazon.

Also, if you have friends or family moving out, remember how much you can help him by recommending this book.

Our link at amazon:

https://www.amazon.com/dp/B084GF14CZ

Our link at Goodreads:

https://www.goodreads.com/book/show/51002306-moving-out-working-abroad-and-keeping-your-sanity

Last but not least, we can keep contact through my page: Levi Borba - Digital Nomad & Expat mentoring www.facebook.com/leviporai

COLLIGERE EXPAT CONSULTANCY

After facing so many questions from expats and those planning to move out, the author of this book founded the company *Colligere Expat Consultancy*.

We help expatriates to solve their doubts, have a stress-free life and give access to some of the best professionals (lawyers, immigration specialists, translators, etc) for very affordable prices.

By purchasing this book, you won a 20-minute consultancy with us for free.

https://expatriateconsultancy.com/

FROM THE SAME AUTHOR

Budget Travelers, Digital Nomads & Expats: The Ultimate Guide: 50 Tips, Tricks, Hacks and Ways to Free Stuff & Cheaper Flights in a Practical Guide to ... (The Digital Nomad & Expat Mentor Book 2)

- **Discover the common opportunity when airlines charge near 70% less for a flight (but still nobody uses it, except their employees)**

- How to pay less when renting an AirBnb

- The hack to not pay for excess luggage.

- The perfect time to look for housing or accommodation and save money.

- The one single phrase to say to a Hotel receptionist give you an upgrade

- How to visit places like the Greek Islands, Cyprus, Malta or Sicily paying 67% less.

- How to make airlines pay a 5-star hotel for you. With Breakfast included!

Buy it in Amazon, here: https://www.amazon.com/dp/B0886KVVMK

Starting Your Own Business Far From Home: What (Not) to Do When Opening a Company in Another State, Country, or Galaxy (The Digital Nomad & Expat Mentor Book 3))

★ **The Business and Non-Business factors to consider when choosing a place to open a company.** *Often neglected, they are the difference between catastrophic failures and remarkable success.*

★ How to find local allies

★ How to understand your competition better than themselves!

★ How to discover and avoid paths leading to business destruction.

★ How to absorb environmental changes and use them in your favor. (Hint: Taleb).

★ **What should you know to not be fooled (avoid the mistakes we made).**

Buy it in Amazon, here: https://

www.amazon.com/dp/B08L1G1D1Q

ABOUT THE AUTHOR

With the knowledge gathered by living and traveling to more than 50 countries, Levi Borba wrote the book that became one of the business travel bestsellers in Amazon: Moving Out, Living Abroad and Keeping your Sanity.

He is also the co-founder of Nearby Airport Hostel Warsaw and Hotelik&Parking Okecie 39. After finishing his studies at the University of Sao Paulo (USP), he was admitted to one of the fiercest management trainee programs of Latin America. There, he spent a year mentored by high-level executives. He relocated to Chile and later to Qatar to join the team of the best airline that humankind has ever created.

After years of development, he moved to Europe. There he took his dreams from paper and started an entrepreneurial venture in the hospitality sector.

In 2020, Levi Borba started a new venture, Colligere Expat Consultancy to help expats and digital nomads have a seamless, stress-free experience abroad.

Check also his Medium profile: https://leviborba.medium.com/

[1] Kahneman, Daniel. Thinking, Fast and Slow. Farrar, Straus and Giroux, 2012.

[1] Survey *Expat Insider* 2018. Link for the complete results: https://www.internations.org/expat-insider/2018/six-types-of-expats-39636

[2] The sum of all numbers in the poll is not 100%.

[3] According to the *CIA The World Factbook*, 88.4% of the population of Qatar are non-Qataris.

[4] Research available at https://geerthofstede.com/culture-geert-hofstede-gert-jan-hofstede/6d-model-of-national-culture/

[5] Other details about culture shock and differences can be found in this article: https://www.expatica.com/moving/integration/how-to-manage-culture-shock-108735/

[6] You can see more details of this story at this link: https://www.mirror.co.uk/tv/tv-news/crown-true-story-behind-princess-20868858

[7] The language I was learning was Polish. It was useful since my next move was to live in Poland.

[8] More about the S.M.A.R.T goals, its benefits and drawbacks at the link: https://www.mindtools.com/pages/article/smart-goals.htm

[9] https://www.dutchnews.nl/features/2015/04/how-to-deal-with-your-aging-parents-when-you-live-abroad/

[10] https://blog.gaijinpot.com/home-isnt-home-anymore/

[11] https://www.bbc.com/worklife/article/20140428-combat-expat-homesickness

[12] Complete article available at https://www.expatica.com/moving/relocation/10-important-tips-for-first-time-expats-450335/

[13] https://www.healthline.com/nutrition/vitamin-d-from-sun

[14] https://www.bbc.com/worklife/article/20140428-combat-expat-homesickness

[15] https://www.qatarliving.com/forum/news/posts/walk-mall-encourages-more-residents-exercise

[16] Full article https://rachelsruminations.com/advice-for-expats/

[17] Elfenbein, H. A., Marsh, A. A., & Ambady, N.; Emotional intelligence and the recognition of emotion from facial expressions, 2002, The Guilford Press.

[18] You can read more about Lera Boroditsky research on how does our language shape the way we think at https://www.edge.org/conversation/lera_boroditsky-how-does-our-language-shape-the-way-we-think

[19] Wittgenstein, Ludwig; *Tractatus Logico-Philosophicus*, 1922, Kegan Paul.

[20] The Pacific Ring is an arc around the Pacific Ocean where many volcanoes, earthquakes and tsunamis are formed. Around three-quarters of the world's dormant and active volcanos are there.

[21]   https://bordeauxexpats.com/2018/06/british-expats-fully-integrated-into-french-culture.html

[22]   You can read some of those examples here   https://www.dailymail.co.uk/home/you/article-2128357/How-french-dream-nightmare.html

[23] Full results of the research made by *Internations* regarding The Best & Worst Countries for Making Friends Abroad can be consulted in https://www.internations.org/press/press-release/the-best-worst-countries-for-making-friends-abroad-39789

[24] Ali, Ilham; Cheva-Isarakul, Janepicha; Kharas, Mark; *A Question of Culture and Belonging: Identity and Integration in Denmark*, Humanity in Action, 2006.

www.ingramcontent.com/pod-product-compliance
Lightning Source LLC
Chambersburg PA
CBHW020600220526
45463CB00006B/2380